COMPSOGNATHUS

by Janet Riehecky
illustrated by Susan Lexa-Senning

THE CHILD'S WORLD

MANKATO, MN

Grateful appreciation is expressed to
Bret S. Beall, Research Consultant,
Field Museum of Natural History, Chicago,
Illinois, who reviewed this book to
insure its accuracy.

Library of Congress Cataloging in Publication Data

Riehecky, Janet, 1953-
    Compsognathus / by Janet Riehecky ; illustrated by Susan Lexa
-Senning.
        p. cm. — (Dinosaur books)
    Summary: Describes both known and hypothesized information about
the dinosaur Compsognathus, including physical appearance and
lifestyle.
    ISBN 0-89565-624-8 (lib. bdg.)
    1. Compsognathus—Juvenile literature.   [1. Compsognathus.
2. Dinosaurs.]   I. Lexa-Senning, Susan, ill.   II. Title.
III. Series: Riehecky, Janet, 1953-   Dinosaur books.
QE862.S3R5334   1990
567.9'7—dc20   90-2512
                                                            CIP
                                                            AC

1 2 3 4 5 6 7 8 9 10 11 12 R 98 97 96 95 94 93 92 91 90

COMPSOGNATHUS

When most people think of dinosaurs,
they think of huge creatures.

4

And many of the dinosaurs *were* enormous.

There were dinosaurs that stood as tall
as a five-story building . . .

and dinosaurs that stretched out as long
as a basketball court.

One type of dinosaur had horns longer
than your legs—and a head almost as big
as a sports car . . .

while others had huge mouths and teeth
as big as your whole hand.

But not every dinosaur was huge. During the time that many of the biggest dinosaurs lived, there also lived the Compsognathus (KOMP-sog-nath-us). The Compsognathus was a tiny dinosaur. In fact, it wasn't much bigger than a chicken!

The largest Compsognathus ever found was only three feet long—and most of that length was just tail. Scientists think it stood only as tall as a person's knee and that it weighed only six to eight pounds. Most cats weigh more than that.

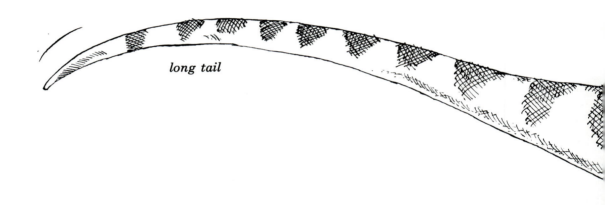

long tail

three main toes; one small side toe

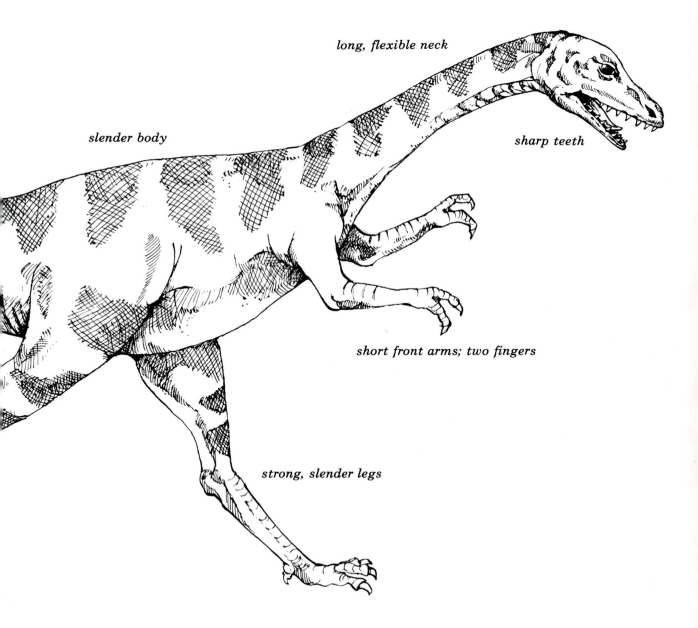

long, flexible neck

slender body

sharp teeth

short front arms; two fingers

strong, slender legs

There were some advantages to being a
tiny dinosaur in a land of giants.

Many big meat eaters were likely to overlook such a small animal. They could feast on thousands of pounds of tasty plant eaters. Why should they bother with one, stringy, little mouthful?

It's also easier to hide when you are little. A tree or a bush was all the Compsognathus needed when it saw a medium-sized meat eater out looking for a light snack.

Of course, it wouldn't be so great to be caught in the path of one of the giant dinosaurs. Some of the really big

dinosaurs could step on a Compsognathus and hardly know it—the way you might step on a large bug.

But the Compsognathus wasn't likely to get stepped on often. Scientists say it was built for speed. It had hollow bones and a slender, streamlined body. It ran on two long, strong, back legs, and its tail helped keep it balanced as it ran. The Compsognathus could zip through the forest, dodging giant dinosaurs with ease.

The Compsognathus needed to be speedy, not only to dodge other dinosaurs, but also to catch its own food. Scientists think the Compsognathus ate such things as insects, frogs, and small lizards. It took speed to catch such quick-moving creatures. One skeleton of a Compsognathus was found with a particularly fast lizard in its stomach. The lizard may have been fast, but the Compsognathus was faster.

The Compsognathus could grab its
lunch with the long fingers on its front
feet. It had only two fingers on each
"hand," but each one had a very long
claw, good for grabbing food.

Once it caught its lunch, the Compsognathus could crunch its victim with its many sharp, pointed teeth. The name Compsognathus means "pretty jaw," but if you were a pterosaur (TAIR-uh-sore), grounded with a broken wing, you wouldn't think those jaws were so pretty.

Scientists don't know a lot about the Compsognathus because they have found only three skeletons of it. And one of those skeletons confused scientists for a while.

In the rock next to the front feet of one Compsognathus, scientists found some hollow areas. These marks in the rock looked like an outline of webbing on the front feet of the Compsognathus. The marks made some scientists think one type of Compsognathus had webbed feet, like a duck. They pictured it paddling around in the lakes or even the ocean.

But as scientists continued to study the skeleton and the rock next to it, they changed their minds. They decided the marks in the rock weren't webbing after all. They were just a part of that kind of rock. So, scientists went back to their first idea about Compsognathus—a speedy, little runner.

It's hard for scientists to learn much about the Compsognathus and the other little dinosaurs because so few of their skeletons are ever found. Many such dinosaurs were probably gulped down whole by big meat eaters. Even if a tiny dinosaur were fossilized, chances are a scientist will not find it. It's just much easier to find a six-foot bone than a two-inch one.

Scientists *have* found a few dinosaurs that were as small, or even smaller, than Compsognathus. The Lesothosaurus (leh-SOTH-uh-sawr-us), an early plant eater, and the Saltopus (SALT-oh-pus), a tiny creature that weighed only two pounds, are two of them. Studying them alongside Compsognathus makes scientists think that any small dinosaur must have been quick and active.

Scientists want to learn all they can about what made tiny dinosaurs special. They would like to learn whether they lived in herds or by themselves. They would like to know how they had babies and whether or not they took care of their babies. They would like to know whether they lived in fear of the big dinosaurs or simply ignored them.

Someday scientists hope to answer these questions. In the meantime, they continue to search for clues. One thing is already known—tiny dinosaurs are just as fascinating as huge ones!

 **Dinosaur Fun**

Wouldn't it be fun to have a hen yard filled with chicken-sized dinosaurs running around? Compsagnathus was not the only small dinosaur. Look at the sizes of the dinosaurs listed below. Use a yardstick and chalk to mark off the size of each dinosaur on a sidewalk (or, for the bigger ones, a driveway). Think about modern-day animals that would fit in that same space.

Protoceratops (pro-to-SAIR-uh-tops) = 6½ feet long, 2½ feet tall

Hypsilophodon (HIP-sih-LOW-fo-don) = 6 feet long, 3 feet tall

Deinonychus (DYE-NON-i-kus) = 8 to 10 feet long, 5 feet tall

Saltopus (SALT-oh-pus) = 2 feet long, 18 inches tall

Fabrosaurus (FAB-roe-SAWR-us) = 3 feet long, 2 feet tall